WHY SHOULD I FORGIVE?

The Power of Forgiveness in a Christian Context

Thelma Melissa Grey

For Stella

CONTENTS

INTRODUCTION

Hurt can run deep, carving scars that seem to never heal. The pain can linger for years, even decades, leaving us bitter and broken. The weight of anger and resentment can become a crushing burden that seems impossible to bear.

But what if there was a way to find healing? What if there was a path to forgiveness, even in the darkest of situations?

This book explores the transformative power of forgiveness in a Christian context, offering hope and healing to those who have been wounded and broken.

PREFACE

The scars from a lifetime of hurts, betrayals, and disappointments had left Mary resentful. She tried to move on, but the pain lingered like a relentless storm cloud, darkening her days and stealing her joy. She knew that forgiveness was the only way to find peace, but the thought of letting go of her anger seemed impossible.

In a world shattered by war, violence, and hatred, John wondered if forgiveness was just a lofty ideal, a naïve dream that could never be achieved. He had seen too much suffering, too much pain, to believe that people could truly let go of their hurt and find healing. But as he encountered stories of forgiveness in the midst of the most unimaginable horrors, he saw the transformative power of forgiveness in a whole new light.

In the depths of his despair, David cried out to God, asking for the strength to forgive the one who had hurt him the most. For years, he had nursed his wounds, nursing his anger and bitterness like a festering wound. But as he embraced the radical call to forgive, he found himself set free from the chains of resentment and bitterness, and filled with a sense of peace he had never known before.

These are the stories of the power of forgiveness in the Christian context. In a world marked by pain and division, they offer a glimmer of hope, a way forward through the darkest of nights.

This book will guide you on a journey of healing, exploring the biblical foundations of forgiveness, the barriers that stand in the way, and the transformative impact of forgiveness in our lives.

CHAPTER 1: FORGIVENESS

Forgiveness is a word that is often heard but seldom understood. For some, it is a simple act of letting go of anger or resentment towards someone who has wronged them. For others, it is a more complex and challenging concept that demands courage, empathy, and vulnerability.

In the Christian context, forgiveness takes on a deeper meaning. It is rooted in the belief that all humans are inherently flawed and that only through the act of forgiveness can we find redemption, healing, and spiritual growth. Forgiveness is at the heart of Christian theology, and it is a central tenet of Christian faith.

The goal of this book is to explore the power of forgiveness. We will examine its biblical foundations, its benefits, and its challenges. Next, we'll look at the barriers that prevent us from forgiving, the steps we can take to overcome them, and the role of forgiveness in healing and reconciliation. We will also explore the impact of forgiveness on personal and spiritual growth, the church, and the world at large.

This book is for anyone who has struggled with forgiveness, who has felt the weight of anger, resentment, and hurt, or who longs for a deeper understanding of the transformative power of forgiveness. Whether you are a lifelong Christian or new to the faith, this book will provide insights, tools, and inspiration to help you cultivate a more forgiving spirit and find the freedom and joy that come with letting go of the past.

The journey of forgiveness is not an easy one. It demands humility, patience, and a willingness to confront our deepest fears and wounds. But as we embark on this journey, we will discover that forgiveness is not just an act of letting go, but a pathway to healing, growth, and transformation. Let us begin.

Defining Forgiveness In The Christian Context

Forgiveness is a big word that has different meanings for different people. In the Christian context, forgiveness means choosing to let go of anger, resentment, and bitterness towards someone who has wronged us. It is an act of grace and mercy that is based on the belief that we are all flawed and in need of forgiveness from God and each other.

Forgiveness does not mean forgetting or excusing the wrong that was done to us. It does not mean that we have to pretend that everything is okay or that we have to trust the person who hurt us again. Forgiveness is not a sign of weakness, nor is it a way to avoid conflict or confrontations.

Instead, forgiveness is a way to find healing, freedom, and peace. When we forgive, we choose to release ourselves from the burden of carrying anger, resentment, and bitterness. We choose to extend grace and mercy to others, just as God has extended it to us. We choose to seek reconciliation and restoration, even if it means setting healthy boundaries and seeking justice for the wrong that was done to us.

In the Christian context, forgiveness is not just a one-time act, but also a process that takes time, effort, and prayer. It requires us to confront our own woundedness, to seek help and support, and to rely on God's strength and guidance. Forgiveness is a journey that leads us to deeper levels of spiritual growth and maturity, as we learn to trust in God's goodness and love.

As Christians, we are called to forgive as we have been forgiven. This means that we choose to extend grace and mercy to others, just as God has extended it to us. It is a challenging and sometimes painful journey, but it is also a journey that leads to freedom, healing, and peace.

The Importance Of Forgiveness In The Christian Faith

Forgiveness is an important part of the Christian faith. It is a central tenet of Christian theology and is woven throughout the Bible. Jesus himself taught the importance of forgiveness, saying in the Lord's Prayer, "Forgive us our debts, as we also have forgiven our debtors" (Matthew 6:12).

The importance of forgiveness in Christian faith is rooted in the belief that God has forgiven us through the sacrifice of Jesus Christ on the cross. We are called to extend that same forgiveness to others, just as God has extended it to us. Forgiveness is not just a nice thing to do; it is a necessary part of our relationship with God and with each other.

Forgiveness is also important for our own spiritual growth and well being. When we hold on to anger, bitterness, and resentment, we carry a heavy burden that can weigh us down and prevent us from experiencing the fullness of God's love and grace. Forgiveness is a way to release us from that burden and find freedom, healing, and peace.

Forgiveness also plays a crucial role in building healthy relationships and communities. When we forgive others, we create space for reconciliation and restoration. We open the door for healing and growth, both for ourselves and for others. Forgiveness allows us to move beyond past hurts and work towards a better future together.

The importance of forgiveness in Christian faith cannot be overstated. It is a way to honor God's love and grace, to find healing and peace, and to build healthy relationships and communities. As Christians, we are called to forgive as we have been forgiven, and in doing so, we bear witness to Christ's love.

The Goal Of This Book

The goal of this book is to help readers understand the power of forgiveness in the Christian context. Forgiveness is a complex and challenging concept that can be difficult to grasp, but it is also essential for personal and spiritual growth.

This book will explore the biblical foundations of forgiveness, its benefits, and its challenges. We will also look at the barriers that prevent us from forgiving, the steps we can take to overcome them, and the role of forgiveness in healing and reconciliation.

The goal of this book is to inspire readers to cultivate a more forgiving spirit in their lives. Whether you are struggling to forgive someone who has hurt you or seeking to deepen your understanding of forgiveness in the Christian context, this book will provide insights, tools, and inspiration to help you on your journey.

Through stories, examples, and practical advice, this book will help readers to see the transformative power of forgiveness in their own lives and in the world around them. We hope that by the end of this book, readers will have a deeper understanding of forgiveness and a greater desire to extend grace and mercy to others, just as God has extended it to us.

CHAPTER 2: BIBLICAL FOUNDATIONS OF FORGIVENESS

The concept of forgiveness has roots in the Bible, and forgiveness is a recurring theme throughout scripture. The story of Joseph in Genesis and the Lord's Prayer are examples of forgiveness in the Old and New Testament, respectively. Jesus models forgiveness in his interactions with people, and forgiveness is presented as an act of grace and mercy. As Christians, we are called to extend that same grace and mercy to others, even when it is painful. This chapter will focus on the benefits of forgiveness and how it can transform our lives and relationships.

Forgiveness In The Old Testament

Forgiveness is a concept that is present throughout the Bible. While the word "forgiveness" is not always used explicitly, the idea of forgiving and being forgiven is present in many Old Testament stories and teachings.

One example of forgiveness in the Old Testament is found in the story of King David and Bathsheba. David, a man after God's own heart, committed adultery with Bathsheba and then had her husband Uriah killed in battle to cover up his sin. When Nathan approached David regarding his wrongdoing, David admitted his fault and sought forgiveness wholeheartedly.
God forgives him, but the consequences of his sin still have an impact on his life and kingdom.

Another example is found in the book of Jonah. Jonah is sent by God to the city of Nineveh to preach repentance, but he resists and tries to run away from God. After a series of events, Jonah finally obeys God and preaches to the people of Nineveh. To Jonah's surprise, the people repent and God forgives them.

The Old Testament also contains teachings about forgiveness. In Leviticus, God commands the Israelites to forgive their neighbors who have wronged them, saying, "Do not seek revenge or bear a grudge against anyone among your people, but love your neighbor as yourself." (Leviticus 19:18)

In the Old Testament, forgiveness is often linked with the idea of repentance and turning away from sin. When people repent and seek forgiveness, God is always ready to extend grace and mercy to them.

While forgiveness is an important concept in the Old Testament, it is fully realized in the person of Jesus Christ and his teachings in the New Testament. In the next chapter, we will explore how Jesus models forgiveness and teaches us to forgive others as we have been forgiven.

Forgiveness In The New Testament

Forgiveness is a central theme in the New Testament, and Jesus Christ is the ultimate model of forgiveness. In his teachings and actions, Jesus shows us the transformative power of forgiveness and the importance of extending grace and mercy to others.

One of the most powerful examples of forgiveness in the New Testament is found in the parable of the prodigal son (Luke 15:11-32). In this story, a younger son asks his father for his inheritance and then squanders it all on reckless living. When he realizes his mistake, he returns home, hoping to be taken back as a servant. Instead, his father runs to greet him, embraces him, and throws a lavish celebration in his honor.

This parable illustrates the love and forgiveness of God towards sinners, and how we too should extend that same love and forgiveness to others.

Jesus also teaches us to forgive others in the Lord's Prayer, where he instructs us to pray, "Forgive us our trespasses, as we forgive those who trespass against us." (Matthew 6:12) This touching prayer serves as a reminder that we are all imperfect and in need of forgiveness. It also calls us to be forgiving and generous in extending that same kindness to others.

In his ministry, Jesus models forgiveness in his interactions with people. When a woman caught in adultery is brought before him, Jesus forgives her and tells her to go and sin no more. (John 8:1-11) When he is dying on the cross, Jesus forgives those who have crucified him, saying, "Father, forgive them, for they know not what they do." (Luke 23:34)

The apostle Paul also emphasizes the importance of forgiveness in his teachings. In Colossians 3:13, he instructs us to

"Bear with each other and forgive one another if any of you has a grievance against someone. Forgive as the Lord forgave you."

In the New Testament, forgiveness is presented as a key component of the Christian faith. It is through forgiveness that we can experience healing and reconciliation with God and with others. In the following chapters, we will explore the benefits of forgiveness and how to cultivate a spirit of forgiveness in our lives.

Jesus' Teachings On Forgiveness

Jesus' teachings on forgiveness are some of the most profound and impactful teachings in the New Testament. He taught that forgiveness is not only a way to reconcile with others but also a way to receive God's forgiveness and experience spiritual healing.

In the Sermon on the Mount, Jesus taught his disciples about the importance of forgiveness. He said, "For if you forgive others their trespasses, your heavenly Father will also forgive you, but if you do not forgive others their trespasses, neither will your Father forgive your trespasses." (Matthew 6:14-15)

This passage highlights the importance of forgiveness as a key component of the Christian faith. Jesus also showed this in his actions, such as when he forgave the paralytic man and healed him (Mark 2:1-12), or when he forgave the woman who anointed his feet with perfume, despite the criticism of those around him (Luke 7:36-50).

Jesus also taught that forgiveness is not just about reconciling with others, but also about cultivating a heart of compassion and mercy. In the parable of the unmerciful servant (Matthew 18:21-35), Jesus teaches we should forgive others as God has forgiven us. He explains that God has forgiven us an immeasurable debt, and therefore we should extend that same forgiveness to others, no matter how great the offense.

Jesus teaches that forgiveness is an ongoing process, and that it is not always easy. In Matthew 18:21-22, Peter asks Jesus how many times he should forgive his brother who sins against him, and Jesus responds, "I do not say to you seven times, but seventy-seven times." This shows that forgiveness is a continual choice, and that it is not always easy.

In summary, Jesus' teachings on forgiveness emphasize its importance as a key component of the Christian faith. Forgiveness is not just about reconciling with others, but also about cultivating a heart of compassion and mercy. It is an ongoing process that requires intentional effort, and it is only through forgiveness that we can experience spiritual healing and reconciliation with God and with others.

The Relationship Between Forgiveness And Salvation

Forgiveness and salvation are intimately connected in the Christian faith. In fact, forgiveness is a prerequisite for salvation. Without forgiveness, we cannot be reconciled to God and experience the fullness of his grace and mercy.

In Ephesians 1:7, Paul writes, "In him we have redemption through his blood, the forgiveness of our trespasses, according to the riches of his grace." This passage highlights the centrality of forgiveness in our salvation. It is through Christ's sacrificial death on the cross that our sins are forgiven, and we are reconciled to God.

Furthermore, forgiveness is not just a one-time event, but also an ongoing process that is necessary for our spiritual growth and maturity. In Colossians 2:13-14, Paul writes, "And you, who were dead in your trespasses and the uncircumcision of your flesh, God made alive together with him, having forgiven us all our trespasses, by canceling the record of debt that stood against us with its legal demands. This he set aside, nailing it to the cross."

This passage highlights the ongoing nature of forgiveness in our lives. It is through Christ's sacrifice that we are forgiven and made alive in him. Our debt has been canceled, and we are no longer held captive by our sins.

Forgiveness is also necessary for our relationships with others. In Matthew 5:23-24, Jesus instructs his disciples to reconcile with others before coming to worship God. He says, "So if you are offering your gift at the altar and there remember that your brother has something against you, leave your gift there before the altar and go. First be reconciled to your brother, and then come and offer your gift."

This passage highlights the importance of forgiveness in our relationships with others. We cannot truly worship God if we are holding onto grudges and bitterness towards others. We must first seek reconciliation and forgiveness before coming to worship him.

Forgiveness and salvation are intimately connected in the Christian faith. Forgiveness is a prerequisite for our salvation, and an ongoing process that is necessary for our spiritual growth and maturity. It is also necessary for our relationships with others and our ability to worship God. It is only through forgiveness that we can experience the fullness of God's grace and mercy in our lives.

CHAPTER 3: THE BENEFITS OF FORGIVENESS

Forgiveness is often seen as a painful process, but it is also incredibly beneficial. In fact, forgiveness has many physical, emotional, and spiritual benefits that can positively impact our lives.

Research has shown that forgiveness can have physical benefits such as lowering blood pressure, decreasing the risk of heart disease, and boosting the immune system. Forgiveness has also been linked to reduced levels of stress and anxiety, which can have a significant impact on overall health and well-being.

Emotionally, forgiveness can lead to increased feelings of happiness, peace, and contentment. It can also help to reduce symptoms of depression and anxiety, as well as improve overall mental health.

Forgiveness is a key aspect of the Christian faith, and it can have many spiritual benefits as well. Forgiving others can help us experience God's grace and mercy more fully, and can bring us closer to Him. Additionally, forgiveness can help us grow in our faith and become more Christ-like, as we learn to love and forgive others as He did.

Forgiveness can also have a significant impact on our

relationships with others. When we forgive those who have wronged us, it can help to rebuild trust and repair damaged relationships. It can also lead to deeper, more meaningful connections with others, as we learn to let go of past hurts and move forward in love and compassion.

Finally, forgiveness can be a powerful tool for personal growth and healing. When we learn to forgive others, it can help us let go of negative emotions and move forward in a more positive and healthy way. Forgiveness can also help us gain a new perspective on difficult situations, and can lead to a greater sense of empathy and understanding towards others.

In this chapter, we have explored some of the many benefits of forgiveness, and how it can positively impact our physical, emotional, and spiritual health, as well as our relationships with others. By learning to forgive, we can experience greater peace, happiness, and personal growth, and become closer to God.

Emotional And Psychological Benefits Of Forgiveness

Forgiveness can have significant emotional and psychological benefits, as it allows us to let go of negative emotions such as anger, bitterness, and resentment. Holding onto these emotions can lead to increased stress, anxiety, and even depression, but forgiveness can help to reduce these symptoms and improve overall mental health.

When we forgive someone, it can also help us feel more in control of our emotions and reactions. We may have initially felt powerless in the face of someone else's actions or words, but choosing to forgive them allows us to take back our power and move forward positively.

Forgiveness can also lead to increased empathy and understanding towards others. When we choose to forgive someone, we acknowledge they are human and flawed, just like we are. This can lead to a greater sense of compassion towards others, as well as a deeper appreciation for the complexity of human relationships.

In addition, forgiveness can be a key component in healing from emotional trauma or abuse. While it is important to acknowledge and work through the pain and hurt caused by such experiences, holding onto anger and bitterness can prevent us from fully moving forward and healing. Choosing to forgive those who have wronged us can be a powerful step in the healing process, allowing us to let go of the negative emotions that are holding us back and moving towards a place of healing and wholeness.

Overall, forgiveness can be a transformative process that can have a significant impact on our emotional and psychological well-being. By letting go of negative emotions and choosing to forgive, we can experience increased happiness, peace, and contentment, as well as greater empathy and understanding towards others.

Physical Health Benefits Of Forgiveness

Forgiveness not only has emotional and psychological benefits but can also have a positive impact on our physical health. Many studies have found that forgiving others can lead to various physical health benefits.

One of the most significant benefits of forgiveness is the reduction of stress. When we hold on to grudges, anger, or resentment, our bodies respond by increasing levels of stress hormones, such as cortisol. This chronic stress can take a toll on our physical health and increase the risk of various diseases such as heart disease, diabetes, and high blood pressure. However, when we choose to forgive, our bodies release tension and reduce stress, leading to lower levels of stress hormones and a decreased risk of these health issues.

Another physical health benefit of forgiveness is a strengthened immune system. Chronic stress can weaken our immune system, making us more susceptible to illnesses and infections. However, studies have found that forgiving others can lead to improved immune system function, and a decreased risk of various illnesses.

In addition, forgiveness can also improve cardiovascular health. Studies have found that forgiving others can lead to lower blood pressure, and a decreased risk of heart disease. Holding onto grudges and resentment can lead to increased inflammation in the body, which can contribute to heart disease. However, by choosing to forgive, we can reduce inflammation and improve heart health.

Finally, forgiveness can also have a positive impact on our sleep. Holding onto anger and resentment can lead to sleep disturbances and insomnia, which can have a negative impact on our physical health. By choosing to forgive and let go of negative emotions, we can improve the quality of our sleep and promote overall physical well-being.

Overall, forgiveness can have many physical health benefits, including reduced stress, improved immune system function, better cardiovascular health, and improved sleep. By choosing to forgive others, we can improve our physical health and promote overall well-being.

Spiritual Benefits Of Forgiveness

Forgiveness is not only beneficial for our emotional and physical well-being but also has important spiritual benefits. In the Christian faith, forgiveness is viewed as a crucial aspect of our relationship with God and our ability to grow in our faith. Here are some of the key spiritual benefits of forgiveness:

<u>Experiencing God's grace and mercy.</u> Forgiving others can help us experience God's grace and mercy more fully. When we forgive others, we are showing the same grace and mercy that God has shown us through the sacrifice of Jesus Christ. This can help us deepen our understanding and appreciation of God's love and forgiveness.

<u>Strengthening our relationship with God</u>. Forgiveness is a key component of our relationship with God. When we hold on to anger and bitterness towards others, it can create a barrier between God and us. By forgiving others, we are opening ourselves up to God's love and allowing Him to work in our lives.

<u>Growing in our faith</u>. Forgiveness can also help us grow in our faith and become more Christ-like. When we forgive others, we are imitating Jesus Christ, who forgave even those who persecuted Him. This can help us develop a deeper understanding of Christ's teachings and become more like Him.

<u>Finding peace and joy.</u> Forgiveness can bring a sense of peace and joy that is difficult to find through any other means. When we let go of anger and bitterness, we free ourselves from the negative emotions that can weigh us down and prevent us from experiencing genuine joy and contentment.

<u>Receiving spiritual blessings</u>. Forgiveness can also lead to spiritual blessings, such as increased wisdom and understanding, a greater sense of purpose, and a closer relationship with God.

By learning to forgive others, we can open ourselves up to these blessings and allow God to work in our lives in powerful ways.

In summary, forgiveness is not only important for our emotional and physical well-being but also has significant spiritual benefits. By learning to forgive others, we can deepen our relationship with God, grow in our faith, find peace and joy, and receive spiritual blessings beyond measure.

Forgiveness As A Means Of Reconciliation

Forgiveness is a powerful tool for reconciliation. When we forgive someone who has wronged us, it can help to repair the relationship and build trust. Forgiveness allows us to let go of negative emotions like anger, bitterness, and resentment, and instead focus on rebuilding the relationship in a positive and healthy way.

Sometimes, forgiveness may even be necessary for reconciliation to occur. For example, if a relationship has been damaged by a conflict or betrayal, forgiveness may be the first step towards healing and restoring the relationship. By extending forgiveness to the person who has wronged us, we open the door for reconciliation and create the opportunity for the relationship to be repaired.

Forgiveness can also be a way to reconcile with ourselves. When we hold on to anger, bitterness, or resentment, it can harm us both emotionally and physically. With forgiveness, we can bid farewell to all the negative emotions and strive ahead with a brighter and healthier outlook. By forgiving ourselves for our mistakes and shortcomings, we can heal and grow as individuals, which can ultimately lead to more fulfilling and meaningful relationships with others.

In the Christian context, forgiveness and reconciliation are linked closely. Jesus teaches we are to forgive others as God has forgiven us, and that we are to seek reconciliation with those we have wronged. By extending forgiveness to others and seeking reconciliation, we can live out our faith and become more Christ-like in our relationships with others.

CHAPTER 4: BARRIERS TO FORGIVENESS

Forgiveness is important in Christianity, but it is not always easy to forgive. Common barriers to forgiveness include anger and resentment, fear of vulnerability, pride and ego, lack of understanding, and past traumas or pain. To overcome these barriers, we must learn to let go of negative emotions, trust in God's grace, love and forgive all people, work on empathy and understanding, and seek professional support if necessary. With patience, prayer, and support, we can learn to forgive and experience greater peace, happiness, and healing.

The Nature Of Hurt And Betrayal

In order to understand the barriers to forgiveness, it is important to first understand the nature of hurt and betrayal. When we are hurt or betrayed by someone we trust, it can be a deeply painful experience. We may feel a range of emotions, including anger, sadness, and disappointment. These emotions can be intense and overwhelming, making it difficult to move on from the hurt and forgive the person who wronged us.

Hurt and betrayal can damage our sense of trust and safety in relationships. When someone we trust betrays us, it can make us question the trustworthiness of others and make it difficult to trust again. This can create a barrier to forgiveness, as we may fear being hurt again if we choose to forgive.

Another factor that can make forgiveness difficult is the perceived injustice of the situation. When we are wronged, we may feel a sense of injustice and a desire for the person who hurt us to face consequences for their actions. This can make it difficult to forgive, as we may feel that forgiving the person would mean letting them off the hook for their wrongdoing.

Finally, our own beliefs and values can create barriers to forgiveness. For example, if we believe that forgiveness means forgetting the hurt or excusing the person who wronged us, we may struggle to forgive. Additionally, if we hold on to anger or bitterness as a way of protecting ourselves or asserting our power, it can make forgiveness difficult.

Hurt and betrayal can be deeply painful experiences that can make forgiveness difficult. Factors such as a damaged sense of trust, a sense of injustice, and our own beliefs and values can create barriers to forgiveness. It is important to understand these barriers and work through them in order to experience the benefits of forgiveness.

The Role Of Anger And Resentment

Anger and resentment are two of the most common emotions associated with the process of forgiveness. When we have been wronged, it is natural to feel resentful towards the person who has hurt us. These emotions can be difficult to manage, and they can make it challenging to forgive.

Anger is a powerful emotion that can be both helpful and harmful. On one hand, anger can motivate us to take action and set healthy boundaries when we have been wronged. It can also help us to release pent-up emotions and process our feelings. However, if anger is not managed effectively, it can lead to negative consequences such as hostility, aggression, and stress.

Resentment, on the other hand, is anger that is directed towards someone who has wronged us in the past. Resentment can be a powerful barrier to forgiveness, as it can keep us stuck in the past and prevent us from moving forward. When we hold on to resentment, we may replay the hurtful event over and over in our minds, which can lead to feelings of bitterness, anger, and even depression.

It is important to acknowledge and work through these emotions as part of the forgiveness process. This may involve expressing our anger and resentment in healthy ways, such as talking to a trusted friend or therapist, journaling, or engaging in physical activity. It may also involve practicing self-compassion and understanding that these emotions are a normal part of the healing process.

Ultimately, forgiveness requires us to let go of our anger and resentment towards the person who has hurt us. This does not mean that we condone their behavior or forget what they have done, but it means that we are willing to release our negative emotions and move forward positively. By doing so, we can experience greater emotional well-being and more fulfilling relationships with others.

The Struggle With Self-Forgiveness

Self-forgiveness can be one of the most challenging aspects of forgiveness. It is often easier to forgive others than it is to forgive ourselves. When we make mistakes, we can be our own harshest critics, replaying the event over and over in our minds, and dwelling on what we should have done differently. This negative self-talk can damage our self-esteem and can make it difficult to move forward.

One reason self-forgiveness can be so challenging is that we hold ourselves to high standards. We expect ourselves to be perfect and to never make mistakes. When we fall short of these expectations, we can feel like we have failed. This sense of failure can be hard to shake, and it can make it difficult to forgive ourselves.

Another barrier to self-forgiveness is shame. When we do something that we regret, we can feel ashamed of ourselves. We may worry that others will judge us or think less of us. This shame can be so intense that we avoid thinking about the situation altogether, which can prevent us from working through our feelings and moving forward.

Fortunately, self-forgiveness is possible. It begins by acknowledging our mistakes and taking responsibility for our actions. We need to recognize that we are human and that making mistakes is a natural part of life. We also need to be kind and compassionate towards ourselves, just as we would be towards a friend who is struggling. This means giving ourselves permission to make mistakes and acknowledging that we are doing the best we can.

Another helpful strategy for self-forgiveness is to reframe the situation. Instead of dwelling on what we did wrong, we can focus on what we learned from the situation and how we can use that knowledge to do better in the future. This can help us let go of the past and move forward with a more positive outlook.

Self-forgiveness can be a challenging but important aspect of the forgiveness process. By acknowledging our mistakes, being kind to ourselves, and reframing the situation, we can learn to forgive ourselves and move forward in a more positive and healthy way.

The Challenge Of Forgiving Those Who Are Unrepentant

Forgiving someone who has wronged us and shown no remorse can be one of the most challenging aspects of forgiveness. It's difficult to let go of anger and resentment towards someone who has hurt us and refuses to take responsibility for their actions. However, it is important to remember that forgiveness is not dependent on the other person's repentance or acknowledgement of their wrongdoing.

One of the key challenges of forgiving the unrepentant is that it may feel like letting them off the hook for their actions. We may worry that forgiving them means we are condoning their behavior or saying that what they did was okay. However, forgiveness is not about excusing or justifying someone's actions, but rather about releasing the negative emotions that are holding us back.

Another challenge of forgiving the unrepentant is that it may feel like we are giving up our power or control in the situation. We may feel like holding onto anger and resentment is the only way to protect ourselves or maintain some sense of justice. However, in reality, holding onto these negative emotions only hurts us in the long run.

It's helpful to remember that forgiveness is ultimately about our own healing and growth, rather than about the other person. When we hold on to anger and resentment, we are allowing the other person's actions to continue to control our lives. By choosing to forgive, we are taking back our power and moving towards a place of healing and wholeness.

Of course, forgiving the unrepentant is difficult, and it may take time and effort to work through the negative emotions that are holding us back. However, with the help of prayer, reflection, and support from others, it is possible to find a path towards forgiveness and healing, even in the most difficult of circumstances.

CHAPTER 5: STEPS TO FORGIVENESS

This chapter provides practical steps to help individuals move towards forgiveness. The first step is acknowledging the pain caused by the other person's actions and allowing oneself to feel the associated emotions. Understanding the underlying causes of the hurt can help individuals gain perspective and empathy towards the other person. Choosing to forgive is a deliberate decision to let go of the hurt and resentment towards the other person, even if they do not deserve it.

Letting go of the hurt may involve a deliberate choice to stop dwelling on the past and to focus on the present and future. Practicing empathy and compassion requires understanding the other person's perspective and situation, which may involve putting oneself in their shoes. Setting healthy boundaries is also an important step in the forgiveness process, as forgiveness does not necessarily mean returning to the same level of relationship with the other person.

Finally, seeking support from friends, family, or a professional can be helpful in navigating the journey towards forgiveness, which can be a challenging process. By following these practical steps, individuals can move towards forgiveness and experience the many benefits it brings.

There are five steps to Forgiveness:
1. Acknowledge the hurt
2. Choose to Forgive
3. Let go of the anger and resentment

4.	Practice empathy and compassion
5.	Seek reconciliation (when possible).

We'll discuss each step in more detail in the next sections.

Acknowledge The Hurt

Acknowledging the hurt is the first step towards forgiveness. It involves allowing one to recognize and feel the emotions associated with the hurt and pain caused by another person's actions. Acknowledging the hurt may be difficult, as it can bring up painful and uncomfortable emotions. However, it is an essential step in the forgiveness process as it allows individuals to work through their emotions and move towards healing.

To acknowledge the hurt, individuals may need to take time to reflect on their feelings and identify the specific actions or words that caused the pain. This may involve journaling, talking to a trusted friend or family member, or seeking the support of a therapist or counselor. It is important to avoid minimizing or dismissing the hurt, as this can prevent individuals from fully working through their emotions and moving towards forgiveness.

Acknowledging the hurt also involves recognizing the impact it has had on one's life and relationships. It can be helpful to identify how the hurt has affected one's thoughts, feelings, and behaviors, as well as how it has impacted relationships with others. This can help individuals gain a deeper understanding of the hurt and its impact, which can be helpful in the forgiveness process.

Acknowledging the hurt is a crucial step towards forgiveness. It involves allowing one to feel the emotions associated with the hurt and recognizing the impact it has had on one's life and relationships. While it can be difficult, acknowledging the hurt is an important step in the journey towards forgiveness and healing.

Choose To Forgive

Choosing to forgive is a crucial step in the forgiveness process. It is a deliberate decision to let go of the hurt and resentment caused by the other person's actions. This decision does not mean that we condone or excuse the behavior, but rather, it means that we are choosing to release ourselves from the negative emotions associated with the hurt.

Choosing to forgive requires a willingness to extend grace and mercy towards the other person, even if they do not deserve it. It may involve recognizing that everyone makes mistakes, and that the other person may struggle with their own issues or challenges. It also involves recognizing that holding onto anger and resentment only hurts us in the long run and can lead to negative physical and emotional health consequences.

Choosing to forgive can be a tough decision, especially if the hurt is deep or the other person has not apologized or taken responsibility for their actions. It may require a significant amount of self-reflection, honesty, and vulnerability to make this choice. However, it is important to remember that forgiveness is a process, and it may take time to fully let go of the hurt and move towards healing.

It is also important to note that forgiveness is a choice that we make for ourselves, and it does not necessarily mean that we will reconcile with the other person or that the relationship will be restored to its previous state. We can choose to forgive while still maintaining healthy boundaries and expectations for the relationship moving forward.

Overall, choosing to forgive is a powerful decision that can lead to greater emotional and psychological well-being, improved relationships, and a more positive outlook on life.

Let Go Of Anger And Resentment

Letting go of anger and resentment is a crucial step in the forgiveness process. When we hold on to these negative emotions, we continue to feel the pain and hurt caused by the other person's actions, and we may even experience physical symptoms such as increased stress and tension.

To let go of anger and resentment, it's important to recognize that forgiveness is a choice. We have the power to choose whether or not we will continue to hold on to these negative emotions. It may not be easy, but it is possible with deliberate effort and intention.

One way to let go of anger and resentment is to practice reframing our thoughts and perspective towards the situation. Instead of focusing on the negative aspects of the situation, we can choose to focus on the positive aspects, such as what we have learned or how we have grown because of the experience.

Another helpful technique is to practice mindfulness and meditation. This involves focusing on the present moment and accepting our thoughts and emotions without judgment. By practicing mindfulness, we can learn to let go of negative emotions and cultivate a sense of peace and calm.

Forgiveness may also involve a willingness to extend grace and mercy to the other person, even if they do not deserve it. This does not mean condoning or excusing their behavior, but rather choosing to let go of the negative emotions associated with the situation.

Letting go of anger and resentment is a crucial step in the forgiveness process. By recognizing that forgiveness is a choice, reframing our thoughts and perspective, practicing mindfulness and meditation, and extending grace and mercy, we can move towards letting go of these negative emotions and experience the freedom and peace that comes with forgiveness.

Practice Empathy And Compassion

Practicing empathy and compassion is a crucial step in the forgiveness process. It involves taking the perspective of the person who hurt us, and trying to understand their situation, motivations, and struggles. By doing so, we can see the situation from a different angle, and develop a sense of empathy towards the other person.

Empathy can be difficult when we are feeling hurt and resentful, but it is important to remember that the other person is also human and capable of making mistakes. By trying to see things from their perspective, we can develop a more nuanced understanding of the situation and the factors that may have contributed to it.

Compassion, on the other hand, involves extending kindness and understanding towards the other person, even if they do not deserve it. It involves a willingness to see the good in the other person, and to extend grace and forgiveness towards them, despite their actions.

Practicing empathy and compassion can be challenging, but it is an important step in the forgiveness process. It can help us move towards a place of understanding and acceptance, and to let go of the anger and resentment that may hold us back. By developing empathy and compassion towards the other person, we can move towards a place of healing and reconciliation.

Seek Reconciliation (When Possible)

Seeking reconciliation can be an important part of the forgiveness process, especially when it is possible and safe to do so. Reconciliation involves restoring the relationship between the parties involved and can help to rebuild trust and repair the damage caused by the hurt.

However, it is important to note that reconciliation is not always possible or even desirable in every situation. In cases where the other person is unrepentant or unwilling to change their behavior, it may not be safe or healthy to pursue reconciliation. In such cases, it may be necessary to focus on the other steps in the forgiveness process, such as letting go of anger and resentment and practicing empathy and compassion.

When reconciliation is possible, it is important to approach the process with a willingness to listen, understand the other person's perspective, and extend grace and forgiveness. This may involve tough conversations and an honest assessment of both parties' roles in the situation.

It is also important to set clear expectations and boundaries for the relationship moving forward. This may involve discussing the changes that need to be made to prevent similar hurts from occurring in the future, as well as outlining the terms of the restored relationship.

Seeking reconciliation can be a challenging and emotional process, but it can also be a powerful step towards healing and growth. By approaching the process with a willingness to listen, understand, and forgive, we can move towards greater understanding, empathy, and connection with others.

CHAPTER 6: FORGIVENESS AND JUSTICE

Forgiveness and justice are two concepts that can seem at odds with each other. Forgiveness involves letting go of anger and resentment towards someone who has caused harm, while justice involves holding people accountable for their actions and ensuring that they face consequences for any harm caused. However, forgiveness and justice are not necessarily mutually exclusive and can coexist in some situations.

Restorative justice is a way forgiveness and justice can align by focusing on repairing the harm caused by an offense, rather than just punishing the offender. By bringing together the victim, offender, and community, restorative justice can provide an opportunity for both forgiveness and justice to be achieved. However, in cases of serious crimes, forgiveness and justice may not align, as forgiveness does not absolve an offender of legal responsibility. It is possible to forgive someone personally while still believing they should face legal consequences.

Forgiveness and justice can also be complicated when the offender does not show remorse or take responsibility for their actions, making forgiveness difficult to achieve, and justice the only means of accountability. Ultimately, forgiveness and justice are complex concepts that can be challenging to reconcile, but restorative justice and a recognition of legal responsibility can promote healing for victims and communities.

The Relationship Between Forgiveness And Justice

Forgiveness and justice are often seen as opposing concepts, but they can actually be closely related. Justice is concerned with fairness and upholding the law, while forgiveness is concerned with releasing the anger and resentment towards the offender. It is important to note that forgiveness does not mean ignoring or condoning the wrongdoing; rather, it is a separate process that can coexist with seeking justice.

Sometimes, seeking justice may be an important step towards forgiveness. For example, in cases of abuse or violence, holding the offender accountable for their actions through legal means can provide a sense of closure and validation for the victim. This can also send a message to society that such actions are not acceptable and may prevent similar offenses from occurring in the future.

On the other hand, forgiveness can also be a powerful tool in promoting justice. When forgiveness is extended to the offender, it can break the cycle of violence and retaliation, leading to a more peaceful and just society. It can also promote empathy and understanding between individuals and communities, fostering a sense of reconciliation and healing.

It is important to note that forgiveness does not mean forgetting or minimizing the wrongdoing. It is a process that requires acknowledging the hurt and pain caused by the offender, while also making a deliberate choice to let go of anger and resentment. Seeking justice and promoting forgiveness can both be important steps towards healing and restoring relationships, whether on an individual or societal level.

The Importance Of Accountability

In forgiveness and justice, accountability plays a crucial role in the process of reconciliation. When someone has caused harm or committed a wrongdoing, it's important that they take responsibility for their actions and are held accountable for the harm they have caused.

Accountability is a necessary step in the process of forgiveness because it acknowledges the harm that has been done and validates the pain and suffering of the victim. It also helps to prevent future harm by ensuring that the offender is held responsible for their actions and takes steps to repair the damage caused.

Accountability can take many forms, including legal consequences, restitution, community service, or simply acknowledging the harm and apologizing to the victim. Whatever form it takes, accountability is an essential component of the forgiveness process because it helps to restore trust and facilitate healing.

However, it's important to note that accountability alone is not sufficient for forgiveness to occur. Forgiveness is a complex process that involves a range of emotional, psychological, and spiritual factors. While accountability may be a necessary component of the process, it does not guarantee forgiveness and should not be used to pressure or manipulate the victim into forgiving.

In some cases, forgiveness may occur without accountability, such as when the offender is no longer alive or cannot be held accountable for their actions. In these situations, the victim may need to find alternative ways to achieve closure and healing.

Accountability is an important component of the forgiveness process, but it should not be seen as a substitute for the complex emotional and spiritual journey of forgiveness. Accountability can help to facilitate healing and prevent future harm, but it must be accompanied by other important factors such as empathy, compassion, and a willingness to let go of anger and resentment.

Restorative Justice As A Form Of Forgiveness

Restorative justice is justice that emphasizes repairing the harm caused by a crime or conflict, rather than simply punishing the offender. It is a process that involves bringing together the victim, the offender, and other affected parties to discuss the harm that was caused and to develop a plan for addressing the harm and restoring relationships.

Restorative justice can be seen as a form of forgiveness because it involves a willingness to move beyond blame and punishment towards healing and reconciliation. Instead of focusing solely on punishing the offender, restorative justice seeks to understand the underlying causes of the harm and to address those causes in a way that promotes healing and growth for all involved.

Restorative justice also emphasizes the importance of accountability. Offenders are required to take responsibility for their actions and to make amends for the harm caused. This may involve apologizing to the victim, making restitution, or engaging in community service.

Restorative justice can be a powerful tool for forgiveness because it allows both the victim and the offender to participate in the healing process. By coming together to discuss the harm caused and to develop a plan for addressing it, both parties can take an active role in the healing process and to work towards reconciliation.

Restorative justice is a form of forgiveness that emphasizes repairing the harm caused by a crime or conflict, rather than simply punishing the offender. It promotes accountability and encourages both the victim and the offender to participate in the healing process. By focusing on healing and reconciliation, restorative justice can be a powerful tool for forgiveness.

Balancing Forgiveness With Healthy Boundaries

Forgiveness is a powerful tool for healing and reconciliation, but it is important to remember that forgiveness does not necessarily mean returning to the same level of relationship with the offender. It is important to set healthy boundaries and expectations for the relationship moving forward.

Setting boundaries involves identifying what behaviors are acceptable and unacceptable, and communicating those boundaries clearly to the offender. This may involve taking steps to protect oneself from future harm, such as limiting contact or ending the relationship entirely. Boundaries also involve holding the offender accountable for their actions and making sure they take responsibility for their behavior.

It is important to remember that setting boundaries does not mean withholding forgiveness. Forgiveness can still be extended even if the relationship is not restored to its previous state. Setting boundaries can actually be a sign of self-respect and self-care, and can help to prevent further harm and promote healing for both parties.

Balancing forgiveness with healthy boundaries can be a difficult and nuanced process, and it may be helpful to seek guidance and support from a trusted friend, family member, or professional. It is important to remember that forgiveness is a personal choice, and there is no one "right" way to navigate the forgiveness process. Ultimately, the goal of forgiveness is to promote healing and growth, both for oneself and for the offender.

CHAPTER 7: FORGIVENESS IN ACTION

The Chapter discusses the practical applications of forgiveness in personal relationships, family dynamics, and professional settings, highlighting that forgiveness is a continuous process that requires effort and intentionality. It provides examples of how forgiveness can be applied, such as setting boundaries, practicing empathy, and letting go of resentment. Self-forgiveness is also emphasized, which involves extending grace and compassion to oneself. The chapter concludes by emphasizing that forgiveness is not a one-size-fits-all solution and requires self-reflection, intentionality, and action towards healing and reconciliation.

Forgiveness In Personal Relationships

Forgiveness is particularly relevant in personal relationships, where hurt and harm can often occur. In these contexts, forgiveness can play a crucial role in repairing and strengthening relationships.

One important aspect of forgiveness in personal relationships is the recognition of mutual responsibility. This means acknowledging that both parties may have contributed to the situation, and both have a role to play in the process of forgiveness. In addition, forgiveness requires vulnerability and a willingness to be open to the other person's perspective and experiences.

Effective communication is also essential in the forgiveness process in personal relationships. This may involve expressing feelings of hurt and pain, listening empathetically to the other person's perspective, and communicating needs and expectations for the future.

It is important to note that forgiveness in personal relationships does not necessarily mean returning to the same level of closeness or trust that existed before the hurt occurred. Setting healthy boundaries and expectations for the relationship moving forward is an important step in the forgiveness process.

Forgiveness can also have a positive impact on personal well-being in relationships. Studies have shown that forgiveness is associated with reduced stress, improved mental health, and increased relationship satisfaction. By practicing forgiveness in personal relationships, individuals can cultivate greater emotional resilience, empathy, and compassion, leading to stronger, more fulfilling relationships.

Forgiveness In Community And Social Contexts

Forgiveness is not only important in personal relationships, but it also has significant implications in community and social contexts. It can play a crucial role in promoting reconciliation, healing, and peace building in situations of conflict and injustice.

One example of forgiveness in a community context is the Truth and Reconciliation Commission (TRC) established in South Africa after apartheid ended. The TRC provided a platform for victims of human rights abuses and their perpetrators to confront and acknowledge the past, seek forgiveness and reconciliation, and work towards a shared future.

Forgiveness can also be important in addressing issues of social injustice and inequality. In situations where groups or individuals have been marginalized or oppressed, forgiveness can provide a pathway towards healing and reconciliation. For example, in the United States, the Civil Rights Movement sought to challenge systemic racism and discrimination, but also emphasized the importance of forgiveness and reconciliation to heal and move forward as a society.

Forgiveness can also be important in promoting social cohesion and reducing conflict in diverse communities. By practicing forgiveness and empathy, individuals can build bridges across divides of race, ethnicity, religion, and culture, and create a sense of shared humanity.

Forgiveness has significant implications in community and social contexts, including promoting reconciliation, addressing issues of social injustice and inequality, and reducing conflict and promoting social cohesion. By practicing forgiveness and empathy, individuals and communities can work towards a more just, peaceful, and compassionate world.

The Role Of Forgiveness In Conflict Resolution

Forgiveness can play a crucial role in conflict resolution, both at a personal and societal level. Conflict arises when there are differences in perspectives, interests, or values, leading to hurt, anger, and resentment. When left unaddressed, conflict can escalate and lead to further damage and harm.

Forgiveness can break this cycle of harm and retaliation by offering a path towards healing and reconciliation. By choosing to forgive, individuals can let go of the hurt and resentment, and focus on finding a resolution that addresses the underlying issues and needs of all parties involved.

In conflict resolution, forgiveness can help to build trust and create a sense of empathy and understanding between the parties. By acknowledging the harm caused, expressing remorse, and asking for forgiveness, individuals can show a willingness to take responsibility for their actions and work towards repairing the relationship.

Restorative justice is one approach to conflict resolution that places a strong emphasis on forgiveness and reconciliation. In restorative justice, the focus is not on punishment, but on repairing the harm caused and restoring relationships. This may involve bringing together the parties involved in a facilitated dialogue, where they can share their perspectives, feelings, and needs, and work towards finding a mutually agreeable solution.

Forgiveness in conflict resolution does not mean overlooking or condoning the harm caused, nor does it require individuals to reconcile or return to the same level of relationship. Rather, forgiveness offers a way to move beyond the hurt and pain, and towards a resolution that addresses the underlying issues and promotes healing and reconciliation.

Examples Of Forgiveness In Action

Forgiveness can take many forms and can be shown in a variety of situations. Here are some examples of forgiveness in action:

1.   A couple in a long-term relationship who have experienced hurt and betrayal may choose to work through their issues and practice forgiveness to move forward in their relationship.
2.   In a community or social context, forgiveness may involve forgiving someone who has wronged you or harmed you. This may involve extending grace and compassion towards the other person, even if they don't deserve it.
3.   Forgiveness can also play a role in conflict resolution, where parties may choose to forgive each other and work towards finding a resolution to their differences. This may involve acknowledging past wrongs and making efforts to move forward in a more positive and constructive manner.
4.   Forgiveness may also be shown in larger societal contexts, such as forgiveness towards those who have committed crimes or acts of violence. This may involve seeking restorative justice, where the focus is on repairing harm and healing relationships rather than solely punishing the offender.

In some cases, forgiveness may involve self-forgiveness, where an individual lets go of self-blame and negative self-talk, and instead extends grace and compassion towards themselves.

Overall, forgiveness in action can take many forms, but the common thread is a willingness to let go of hurt and resentment, and to extend grace and compassion towards oneself and others.

CHAPTER 8: LIVING A FORGIVING LIFE

In this chapter, we will explore the concept of living a forgiving life. Forgiveness is not just a one time event or a temporary state of mind, but a way of life that can bring lasting peace and fulfillment. Living a forgiving life involves cultivating a mindset of forgiveness, practicing forgiveness in our daily lives, and making forgiveness a core value in our relationships and interactions with others.

Cultivating a mindset of forgiveness involves adopting a perspective of compassion and empathy towards others, recognizing the inherent worth and dignity of all people, and acknowledging our own flaws and mistakes. This mindset allows us to see beyond the surface-level actions of others and to understand the deeper motivations and struggles that may drive their behavior.

Practicing forgiveness in our daily lives involves intentionally seeking opportunities to extend grace and mercy towards others, even in small and seemingly insignificant ways. This may involve offering a kind word or gesture to someone who has wronged us, choosing to let go of a minor offense, or intentionally seeking out opportunities to serve and support others.

Making forgiveness a core value in our relationships and interactions with others involves setting expectations for ourselves and others that prioritize forgiveness and reconciliation. This may involve actively seeking ways to resolve conflicts and repair relationships, being willing to apologize and seek forgiveness when we have wronged others, and making a commitment to consistently extend grace and mercy towards others.

Living a forgiving life requires intentional effort and a willingness to prioritize forgiveness in all areas of our lives. By cultivating a mindset of forgiveness, practicing forgiveness in our daily lives, and making forgiveness a core value in our relationships and interactions with others, we can experience the many benefits of forgiveness and live a life that is marked by peace, joy, and fulfillment.

The Importance Of Ongoing Forgiveness

Forgiveness is not a one time event, but rather an ongoing process. It's important to recognize that even after we have decided to forgive someone, we may still experience negative emotions and memories related to the hurt they caused us. Additionally, new situations or interactions may arise that challenge our ability to continue extending forgiveness.

Living a forgiving life involves being aware of these ongoing challenges and making a conscious effort to continue practicing forgiveness. This may involve:

1. Practicing self-forgiveness: Just as we need to forgive others, it's important to extend the same grace and mercy to ourselves when we make mistakes or fall short of our own expectations.

2. Cultivating a forgiving mindset: Adopting a mindset of forgiveness can help us approach situations with empathy, compassion, and a willingness to extend grace.

3. Letting go of grudges: Holding onto grudges and resentment only serves to harm ourselves. Letting go of these negative emotions can free us to live a more positive and fulfilling life.

4. Practicing empathy and understanding: Seeking to understand the perspectives and experiences of others can help us approach situations with greater compassion and empathy.

5. Maintaining healthy boundaries: Forgiveness does not necessarily mean returning to the same level of relationship or interaction with the other person. It's important to establish and maintain healthy boundaries to protect ourselves from future harm.

Overall, living a forgiving life requires ongoing effort

and a commitment to approaching situations with empathy, understanding, and grace. By cultivating a forgiving mindset and practicing ongoing forgiveness, we can experience greater peace, joy, and fulfillment in our relationships and daily lives.

How To Cultivate A Forgiving Spirit

Cultivating a forgiving spirit is an ongoing process that requires intentional effort and practice. Here are some ways to cultivate a forgiving spirit:

1. Practice self-reflection: Take time to reflect on your own actions and behavior. Identify areas where you may have hurt others and seek to make amends.

2. Practice gratitude. Gratitude can help shift our perspective towards forgiveness. Focus on the positive aspects of your life and relationships, rather than dwelling on the negative.

3. Practice empathy. Seek to understand and empathize with others, even when their actions may have caused you pain. Try to put yourself in their shoes and consider their perspective.

4. Practice forgiveness daily. Make a deliberate effort to practice forgiveness in your daily interactions with others. This may involve letting go of minor offenses or showing grace and mercy towards others.

5. Surround yourself with forgiveness. Surround yourself with people who embody forgiveness and encourage a forgiving spirit in others. Seek out books, podcasts, or other resources that promote forgiveness.

6. Let go of resentment. Resentment can be a barrier to forgiveness. Practice letting go of resentment by reframing your thoughts towards the situation and focusing on the present and future, rather than dwelling on the past.

7. Practice self-care. Taking care of your own physical, emotional, and mental well-being can help cultivate a forgiving spirit. This may involve exercise, meditation, therapy, or other self-care practices.

Cultivating a forgiving spirit requires ongoing effort and practice. By practicing self-reflection, gratitude, empathy, forgiveness, surrounding yourself with forgiveness, letting go of resentment, and practicing self-care, you can cultivate a forgiving spirit and experience the many benefits it brings.

Practicing Forgiveness As A Christian Discipline

Practicing forgiveness is an essential discipline for Christians. The Bible teaches that forgiveness is not just a nice thing to do but also a commandment. In the Lord's Prayer, Jesus teaches us to pray, "Forgive us our debts, as we also have forgiven our debtors." (Matthew 6:12) Furthermore, Jesus himself modeled forgiveness throughout his life, including forgiving those who crucified him.

To cultivate a forgiving spirit as a Christian, one can begin by acknowledging our own need for forgiveness from God. When we understand the depth of our own sin and the mercy God has shown us, it becomes easier to extend forgiveness to others.

Another way to cultivate a forgiving spirit is by meditating on God's Word and the example of Christ. Reading and reflecting on passages such as Colossians 3:13, "Bear with each other and forgive one another if any of you has a grievance against someone. Forgive as the Lord forgave you," can inspire us to forgive others as Christ has forgiven us.

Prayer is also an important part of cultivating a forgiving spirit. Praying for the person who has hurt us and asking for the strength to forgive them can help soften our hearts and release the burden of resentment and anger.

Finally, it's important to remember that forgiveness is not a one time event but an ongoing process. We may need to forgive the same person multiple times or forgive different people for different offenses. As we continue to practice forgiveness, we can experience the freedom and peace that comes with letting go of anger and bitterness.

The Impact Of Forgiveness On Personal And Spiritual Growth

Forgiveness can have a profound impact on personal and spiritual growth. It allows individuals to let go of negative emotions and move towards a place of healing and growth. By forgiving others, individuals can experience a sense of liberation from resentment, anger, and bitterness, leading to increased levels of happiness, inner peace, and contentment.

Forgiveness can also lead to greater spiritual growth. In many religious traditions, forgiveness is seen as a virtue and a means of attaining a closer relationship with a higher power. By extending forgiveness, individuals are able to align themselves with the values of compassion, empathy, and love that are central to many spiritual practices.

Furthermore, forgiveness can help individuals to grow and develop in a number of ways. It can foster a greater sense of self-awareness and empathy towards others, leading to more meaningful and fulfilling relationships. It can also help individuals to become more resilient in the face of adversity, by providing them with the ability to bounce back from challenging situations and experiences.

Finally, forgiveness can be a powerful tool for personal transformation. By releasing negative emotions and embracing forgiveness, individuals are able to create space for growth, healing, and self-discovery. It can be a catalyst for positive change, leading individuals to live more meaningful and purposeful lives.

Forgiveness has a transformative effect on personal and spiritual growth. By cultivating a forgiving spirit, individuals are able to experience increased levels of happiness, inner peace, and contentment, as well as greater self-awareness, empathy, and resilience. It can be a powerful tool for personal transformation, leading individuals to live more meaningful and purposeful lives.

CHAPTER 9: FORGIVENESS AND THE CROSS

This chapter explores the concept of forgiveness within the Christian faith and its relationship to the death and resurrection of Jesus Christ. According to Christian doctrine, Jesus' death on the cross is seen as a sacrifice that allows for the forgiveness of sins. Through Jesus' sacrifice, Christians believe that they can be reconciled with God and experience eternal life.

The chapter highlights how the act of forgiveness is central to the Christian faith and is seen as a fundamental part of following Jesus' example. Christians are called to forgive others as God has forgiven them. The chapter emphasizes the importance of forgiveness not only in personal relationships but also in larger social and community contexts.

The chapter also discusses the role of the cross in understanding forgiveness. Jesus' death on the cross is seen as a demonstration of love and forgiveness towards humanity. Through the cross, Christians are called to emulate this same spirit of forgiveness and love towards others.

The chapter also explores the idea of substitutionary atonement, which is the belief that Jesus' death on the cross was a substitution for the punishment that humanity deserved for their sins. This belief is central to the Christian understanding of forgiveness and provides a framework for understanding the importance of forgiveness in Christian life.

Overall, the chapter emphasizes the importance of forgiveness in the Christian faith and the role of the cross in understanding and practicing forgiveness. It highlights the transformative power of forgiveness and the impact it can have on personal and spiritual growth.

The Significance Of Forgiveness In The Context Of The Cross

In the context of Christianity, the concept of forgiveness is deeply rooted in the message of the Cross. The Bible teaches that all human beings have sinned and fallen short of the glory of God, and that the punishment for sin is death (Romans 3:23, 6:23). However, God, in His love and mercy, provided a way for humanity to be reconciled to Him through the sacrifice of His Son, Jesus Christ, on the Cross.

Through the Cross, Jesus bore the punishment for the sins of all humanity and offered the gift of forgiveness to anyone who would repent and turn to Him in faith. As Jesus hung on the Cross, He spoke the words, "Father, forgive them, for they do not know what they are doing" (Luke 23:34). This act of forgiveness demonstrated the depth of God's love for humanity and His willingness to forgive even the most heinous of sins.

For Christians, the message of the Cross is a call to live a life of forgiveness, just as Christ forgave us. In the Lord's Prayer, Jesus taught his followers to pray, "Forgive us our debts, as we also have forgiven our debtors" (Matthew 6:12). This prayer reminds us that our forgiveness is intimately tied to our willingness to forgive others.

Furthermore, the Cross also teaches us that forgiveness is not cheap. It comes at a great cost, and it requires us to confront the reality of our own sinfulness and need for forgiveness. To live a life of forgiveness, we must be willing to extend grace and mercy to others, even when it is difficult or uncomfortable.

Ultimately, the message of the Cross reminds us that forgiveness is a fundamental aspect of the Christian faith. It is through forgiveness that we are reconciled to God and to one another, and it is through forgiveness that we are able to live a life of love and compassion towards others.

Jesus' Ultimate Act Of Forgiveness

In the context of Christianity, the ultimate act of forgiveness is seen in Jesus Christ's death on the cross. Christians believe that Jesus, the Son of God, came to earth to die for the sins of humanity, offering forgiveness and reconciliation between God and humanity.

The concept of forgiveness is central to the Christian faith and is exemplified in Jesus' words and actions throughout his life. For instance, Jesus taught his disciples to forgive those who wronged them, and he demonstrated this in his interactions with others, including forgiving the woman caught in adultery and praying for those who crucified him.

However, Jesus' ultimate act of forgiveness was seen in his death on the cross. Christians believe that Jesus, being without sin, willingly took on the punishment that humanity deserved, bearing the weight of our sins on the cross. In doing so, he made a way for forgiveness and reconciliation between God and humanity, bridging the gap that sin had created.

The significance of forgiveness in the context of the cross is not only about receiving forgiveness but also extending it to others. Christians are called to follow Jesus' example and forgive others, just as he has forgiven them. This includes forgiving those who have wronged us, letting go of resentment and anger, and seeking reconciliation when possible.

Overall, the significance of forgiveness in the context of the cross is a powerful reminder of the depth of God's love for humanity and the transformative power of forgiveness. It reminds us that forgiveness is not just a personal matter, but it has the potential to heal relationships, restore communities, and bring about reconciliation between humanity and God.

Substitutionary Atonement

Substitutionary atonement is a central doctrine in Christian theology that explains the nature and purpose of Jesus' death on the cross. At its core, substitutionary atonement teaches that Jesus took the place of sinful humanity and bore the punishment that we deserved for our sins.

According to this doctrine, humanity is fundamentally flawed and separated from God due to sin. Our rebellion against God has created a barrier between us and Him, preventing us from having a relationship with our Creator. The Bible teaches that the penalty for sin is death, both physical and spiritual. In other words, sin leads to eternal separation from God.

However, God in His mercy and love chose to offer a way for humanity to be reconciled to Him. He sent His Son, Jesus, to take on human form and live a sinless life. By doing so, Jesus was able to offer Himself as a sacrifice for the sins of all humanity.

On the cross, Jesus took upon Himself the punishment that we deserved for our sins. He suffered and died in our place, bearing the weight of our guilt and shame. In this act of self-sacrifice, Jesus satisfied the justice of God and made it possible for us to be forgiven and reconciled to God.

Through faith in Jesus and His sacrificial death, we can receive forgiveness for our sins and be restored to a right relationship with God. This is the heart of the gospel message, and it is the hope that Christians hold onto.

Substitutionary atonement has been a controversial topic throughout the history of Christianity, with various theologians and scholars offering different interpretations of the doctrine. However, at its core, it remains a powerful reminder of the depth of God's love and the incredible sacrifice that Jesus made on behalf of humanity.

The Power Of The Cross To Transform Hearts And Relationships

The Cross is a powerful symbol of forgiveness in the Christian faith. It represents the ultimate act of love and forgiveness, as Jesus willingly gave his life to reconcile humanity with God. Through his death on the Cross, Jesus paid the price for the sins of all people, offering forgiveness and the opportunity for a new life.

Jesus' ultimate act of forgiveness is an example for all believers to follow. As Christians, we are called to forgive others as Christ has forgiven us. This can be a challenging and ongoing process, but it is through the power of the Cross that we are able to find the strength and grace to do so.

The message of the Cross is not just about forgiveness between humanity and God, but also about forgiveness between individuals. Jesus taught his followers to love their enemies, bless those who curse them, and pray for those who mistreat them. This radical approach to forgiveness goes against the natural human tendency to hold onto anger and resentment, and instead encourages a spirit of compassion and empathy towards others.

Through the power of the Cross, individuals and relationships can be transformed. The act of forgiveness can lead to healing and restoration, and can pave the way for a brighter future. When we forgive others, we are not only releasing them from our anger and resentment, but we are also freeing ourselves from the burden of bitterness and pain.

The power of the Cross is a reminder of the transformative and life-giving nature of forgiveness. As Christians, we are called to follow Jesus' example of forgiveness and love, and to extend grace and mercy to those who have wronged us. Through the power of the Cross, we can find the strength and courage to forgive and move towards a brighter future.

CHAPTER 10: FORGIVENESS AND THE CHURCH

This chapter explores the role of forgiveness in the Church. The Church is a community of believers that is grounded in forgiveness, and as such, forgiveness should be a central aspect of the Church's mission and ministry.

The chapter discusses how forgiveness can be expressed within the Church community in various ways, including through confession, communion, and prayer. Confession allows individuals to acknowledge their sins and seek forgiveness from God and the community. Communion, as a sacrament, reminds Christians of Christ's sacrifice and forgiveness, and it can serve as a time for reflection and renewal. Prayer can also be a powerful tool for forgiveness, both in seeking forgiveness and in offering forgiveness to others.

The chapter also highlights the importance of forgiveness in the context of church leadership and pastoral care. Church leaders have a responsibility to model forgiveness and to create an environment that fosters forgiveness and reconciliation. Pastoral care involves providing support and guidance to individuals who are struggling with forgiveness, and this can involve helping individuals to navigate the forgiveness process and providing resources and support.

Furthermore, the chapter examines the challenges that can arise in forgiveness within the Church community. These challenges include situations where forgiveness is not offered or received, conflicts between individuals, and instances of abuse or harm. In such situations, the Church has a responsibility to address the harm and seek justice while also promoting forgiveness and reconciliation.

Overall, the chapter emphasizes that forgiveness is a crucial aspect of the Church's mission and ministry. By fostering a culture of forgiveness, the Church can promote healing, reconciliation, and spiritual growth within the community.

The Role Of Forgiveness In The Life Of The Church

Forgiveness plays a central role in the life of the church. It is a key aspect of Christian teaching and a foundational practice for believers. The church is called to be a community of forgiveness, where members are called to forgive one another as Christ has forgiven them.

One of the primary ways in which forgiveness is practiced in the church is through the sacrament of reconciliation. This sacrament involves confessing one's sins to a priest and receiving absolution, or forgiveness, from God. It is a powerful way for individuals to experience the forgiveness of God and to be reconciled to the church community.

Another way in which forgiveness is practiced in the church is through the practice of confession and forgiveness among members. The church is called to be a community of accountability, where members hold one another accountable for their actions and offer forgiveness when necessary. This can involve confessing sins to one another and seeking forgiveness, as well as extending forgiveness to others who have wronged us.

The church is also called to extend forgiveness to those outside of the church community. This can involve reaching out to those who are marginalized or oppressed, offering forgiveness to those who have wronged us, and seeking reconciliation with those with whom we have been in conflict.

Ultimately, the church is called to be a community of forgiveness that reflects the forgiveness and love of Christ. Through the practice of forgiveness, the church can demonstrate the transformative power of God's love and help to bring healing and reconciliation to individuals, families, and communities.

Addressing Conflict And Division Within The Church

Addressing conflict and division within the church is a crucial aspect of promoting forgiveness and unity within the body of believers. The Bible instructs us to be peacemakers and to seek reconciliation with our brothers and sisters in Christ (Matthew 5:9, Matthew 18:15-17, Ephesians 4:3). Therefore, it is important for the church to have processes in place for addressing conflict in a healthy and productive manner.

One approach is to promote open communication and dialogue between parties involved in the conflict. This may involve having a mediator or counselor who can facilitate the conversation and help parties to listen to one another, express their concerns, and work towards a resolution. The goal is to identify common ground and to find a way forward that honors the concerns and needs of all parties involved.

Another approach is to encourage forgiveness and reconciliation through the practice of confession and repentance. This involves acknowledging one's own role in the conflict, seeking forgiveness from those who have been harmed, and making a commitment to change behavior moving forward. This approach promotes humility and self-reflection, and it can help to rebuild trust and foster a sense of unity within the church.

It is also important for the church to model forgiveness and reconciliation at all levels, from leadership down to individual members. This can be done through preaching and teaching on forgiveness, sharing stories of forgiveness and reconciliation within the church community, and promoting a culture of grace and compassion. When forgiveness is actively practiced and modeled within the church, it can have a transformative impact on individuals and the wider community, fostering healing, growth, and unity.

The Importance Of Forgiveness In Christian Witness

In Chapter 10, the focus is on the role of forgiveness in the life of the church, specifically in relation to Christian witness. The church is called to be a community of love and forgiveness, as exemplified by Jesus Christ. Forgiveness is not just a personal matter, but also a communal one, as conflicts and divisions can arise within the church.

When conflicts arise, the church is called to address them with humility, grace, and a commitment to reconciliation. This involves acknowledging and addressing any wrongdoing, offering and receiving forgiveness, and working towards restoration and healing.

Forgiveness within the church is not just about resolving conflicts, but also about embodying the message of the gospel. As Christians, we are called to love and forgive one another, even when it is difficult or costly. This witness to forgiveness can be a powerful testimony to the transformative power of the gospel in the world.

However, forgiveness in the church is not always easy. It may require confronting difficult truths, admitting fault, and relinquishing the desire for revenge or retribution. But when the church is committed to forgiveness, it can be a powerful force for reconciliation, healing, and transformation in the world.

CHAPTER 11: FORGIVENESS IN THE WORLD

This chapter explores the importance of forgiveness in the world, including its potential to transform relationships, communities, and even nations. The chapter provides examples of forgiveness in action, such as the Truth and Reconciliation Commission in South Africa and the story of Rwandan genocide survivor Immaculée Ilibagiza. Forgiveness in the world also involves working towards social justice and systemic change to address the root causes of injustice and promote fairness and equality. The chapter emphasizes that forgiveness on a global scale can be challenging but has the potential for healing and reconciliation.

Forgiveness And Global Conflicts

Forgiveness can play an important role in resolving global conflicts. While it is not a simple solution, forgiveness can promote understanding, empathy, and reconciliation between individuals, groups, and nations.

One example of forgiveness in the context of global conflict is the Truth and Reconciliation Commission in South Africa, which sought to address the injustices of apartheid. The commission provided a forum for victims to share their stories and for perpetrators to acknowledge their actions and seek forgiveness. While the process was not without its challenges and criticisms, it was seen as a significant step towards healing and reconciliation in South Africa.

Another example is the work of peace building organizations, which often emphasize the importance of forgiveness and reconciliation in resolving conflicts. These organizations often bring together individuals from opposing sides of a conflict to engage in dialogue, share their stories, and seek understanding and empathy for one another.

Forgiveness can also be seen in the work of human rights advocates and organizations, who seek to address past and ongoing injustices and promote healing and reconciliation between individuals and communities. By acknowledging the pain and suffering caused by past wrongs and working towards forgiveness and reconciliation, these organizations aim to create a more just and peaceful world.

In all these examples, forgiveness is not an easy or quick solution, but rather a long and difficult journey towards healing, reconciliation, and peace. However, forgiveness can be a powerful force for transformation and can help to break the cycle of violence and injustice that can perpetuate global conflicts.

The Role Of Forgiveness In Peacebuilding

Forgiveness can play a crucial role in peacebuilding efforts around the world. In many cases, conflicts arise due to deep-rooted grievances and hurts that have been inflicted by one group on another. These grievances can be so severe that it seems impossible for the two sides to ever reconcile or forgive one another.

However, forgiveness can break through this cycle of violence and retaliation, allowing for the possibility of peace and reconciliation. When individuals or groups are able to forgive one another, they can begin to build trust and work towards common goals.

One approach to peacebuilding through forgiveness is called "restorative justice." This approach emphasizes the importance of repairing harm that has been done, rather than just punishing the perpetrator. It involves bringing together the victim, the offender, and the community to work towards repairing the harm that has been done and restoring relationships.

Another way that forgiveness can play a role in peacebuilding is through reconciliation efforts. Reconciliation involves acknowledging past wrongs and working towards restoring broken relationships. It requires a willingness to listen to the other side, to empathize with their pain, and to take steps to make things right.

Overall, forgiveness is an essential component of peacebuilding efforts, as it can help to break down barriers and foster relationships built on trust and understanding. It requires humility, empathy, and a commitment to healing past hurts, but the rewards can be tremendous, as communities and nations move towards lasting peace and reconciliation.

Forgiveness As A Response To Injustice And Violence

Forgiveness as a response to injustice and violence is a complex and controversial topic, and opinions vary widely. Some people argue that forgiveness is necessary for healing and moving forward after a traumatic event, while others argue that forgiveness can be harmful or even impossible in certain situations.

One perspective is that forgiveness can be a powerful tool for victims of injustice and violence to regain a sense of control and agency in their lives. By forgiving their oppressors, victims can refuse to be defined by the harm they have suffered and can choose to move forward with their lives in a positive direction. Forgiveness can also promote healing and emotional wellbeing, reducing the long-term effects of trauma.

However, others argue that forgiveness is not always appropriate or even possible in cases of extreme injustice or violence. Some argue that forgiveness can be used as a tool of oppression, forcing victims to reconcile with their oppressors before justice has been served. Others argue that forgiveness is a personal choice and that victims should not be pressured to forgive if they are not ready or willing to do so.

It is important to recognize that forgiveness is a complex issue and that there is no one-size-fits-all approach. Each individual and situation is unique, and the decision to forgive should be made based on a careful consideration of the circumstances and the needs and feelings of those involved. Ultimately, forgiveness should never be used as a way to avoid or minimize the responsibility of those who have committed harm, but rather as a way to promote healing and reconciliation.

CHAPTER 12: FORGIVENESS AND HEALING

Chapter 12 of the book on Forgiveness and Healing explores the connection between forgiveness and healing, both physically and emotionally. Forgiveness can release negative emotions and promote inner peace, leading to improved mental health and a stronger immune system. The chapter also discusses forgiveness in the context of chronic illness and collective trauma, highlighting its transformative power in promoting healing and reconciliation. While forgiveness is not a one-size-fits-all solution, it is ultimately a path towards greater peace, compassion, and understanding.

Forgiveness As A Pathway To Healing

Forgiveness has the power to bring healing to wounded hearts and broken relationships. When we hold onto grudges, bitterness, and resentment, we carry emotional and spiritual baggage that can weigh us down and hinder our ability to move forward. However, when we choose to forgive, we release ourselves from the grip of these negative emotions and open ourselves up to the possibility of healing.

Forgiveness can be a difficult and painful process, especially when the wounds are deep and the hurt is severe. But by choosing to forgive, we allow ourselves to acknowledge the pain and hurt, process the emotions associated with the experience, and move towards healing and wholeness. By extending forgiveness, we also create space for the possibility of reconciliation, which can be a powerful catalyst for healing and restoration.

Forgiveness is not a one-time event but rather an ongoing process that requires intentional effort and commitment. It involves letting go of the desire for revenge or retribution and instead choosing to extend compassion, empathy, and grace towards the person who has caused harm. It can also involve setting healthy boundaries to protect oneself from future harm while still extending forgiveness and seeking healing.

As Christians, we look to Jesus as the ultimate model of forgiveness and healing. Through his sacrificial love on the cross, he offers forgiveness and redemption to all who come to him in faith. In his ministry, he also demonstrated a deep concern for the physical, emotional, and spiritual healing of those he encountered. As we follow Jesus' example, we can choose to extend forgiveness and seek healing for ourselves and those around us, trusting in God's grace and power to bring wholeness and restoration to all areas of our lives.

The Relationship Between Forgiveness And Emotional And Physical Health

The act of forgiveness has been found to have a significant impact on emotional and physical health. Holding onto grudges and anger can lead to stress, anxiety, and depression, which can then manifest in physical health issues such as high blood pressure, heart disease, and weakened immune systems. By contrast, forgiving others has been linked to increased feelings of happiness, inner peace, and improved relationships.

Research has also shown that forgiveness can lead to a decrease in negative emotions such as anger, resentment, and hostility. This reduction in negative emotions can then have a ripple effect on other aspects of life, such as improved sleep, decreased pain, and a reduction in symptoms of anxiety and depression.

One reason for this positive impact on health is that forgiveness allows individuals to let go of negative emotions and move forward with a sense of purpose and meaning. It can also promote greater empathy and compassion, which can lead to stronger relationships and a greater sense of social support.

While forgiveness may not always lead to a complete resolution of a situation, it can provide a pathway to healing and allow individuals to find closure and peace. By choosing to forgive, individuals can break free from the cycle of anger and hurt and move towards a more positive and fulfilling life.

Stories Of Forgiveness And Healing

Stories of forgiveness and healing abound, showing the profound impact that forgiveness can have on a person's emotional, spiritual, and physical well-being.

Here are some of them:

- Azim Khamisa. His son was murdered by a 14-year-old boy in a gang initiation. Rather than seeking revenge, Khamisa founded the Tariq Khamisa Foundation to educate young people about the consequences of violence and promote forgiveness and empathy. Khamisa's act of forgiveness led to a reconciliation with the boy's grandfather, who had played a role in raising the boy in a gang culture.
- Eve Ensler. Eve is the author of The Vagina Monologues, who was sexually abused by her father as a child. Ensler's journey to forgiveness involved confronting her father and ultimately finding compassion for him as a wounded human being. Through her work as a writer and activist, Ensler has helped many other survivors of sexual violence find healing and empowerment.
- Immaculée Ilibagiza. Immaculée was a survivor of the Rwandan genocide, who proved the power of forgiveness to heal even the deepest wounds. After hiding for months in a small bathroom with several other women, Ilibagiza emerged to find that her entire family had been killed. Through her deep faith and the practice of prayer and forgiveness, Ilibagiza was able to transcend her trauma and find a sense of peace and purpose in her life. Today, she is a bestselling author and speaker who travels the world sharing her message of forgiveness and healing.
- Nelson Mandela. Nelson Mandela spent 27 years in prison, much of it in solitary confinement, for his efforts to end apartheid in South Africa. When he was released in

1990, he famously forgave his captors and worked towards reconciliation and healing in his country. His forgiveness and leadership paved the way for a peaceful transition to democracy in South Africa.

• The Amish community in Nickel Mines. In 2006, a gunman entered a one-room schoolhouse in Nickel Mines, Pennsylvania, and opened fire on the children inside. Five children were killed, and several others were injured. The Amish community, known for their commitment to forgiveness and nonviolence, immediately forgave the shooter and his family. They even attended the shooter's funeral to offer their condolences and support to his family.

• Eva Kor. Eva Kor was a survivor of the Holocaust who suffered horrific abuse at the hands of Nazi doctors at the Auschwitz concentration camp. Despite the trauma she endured, Eva forgave her abusers and worked towards healing and reconciliation. She founded the CANDLES Holocaust Museum and Education Center to promote healing and forgiveness, and she even traveled to Germany to meet with one of the doctors who had experimented on her.

• Eric Smallridge. Eric Smallridge was a young man who caused a drunk driving accident that killed two sisters, Ileana and Jacqueline Cruz. While he was serving time in prison, he reached out to the Cruz family to ask for their forgiveness. The family eventually forgave him and even campaigned for his early release from prison. Smallridge went on to become an advocate for responsible drinking and spoke about his experience in schools and community groups.

• Thich Nhat Hanh. Thich Nhat Hanh is a Vietnamese Buddhist monk and peace activist who was exiled from his home country during the Vietnam War. Despite the trauma he experienced, Thich Nhat Hanh worked towards forgiveness and reconciliation between the Vietnamese and American people. He founded the Plum Village community, a meditation center in France, and has written extensively about the power of forgiveness and compassion in promoting healing and peace.

These stories and many others demonstrate that forgiveness is not only a moral imperative but also a key to personal and collective healing. By choosing forgiveness, we can transform our pain and trauma into opportunities for growth, compassion, and service to others.

CHAPTER 13: CONCLUSION

In summary, forgiveness is a complex and transformative concept that can bring healing, growth, and reconciliation. It is a process that requires intentionality, effort, and commitment. As Christians, forgiveness is not only a personal practice but also a call to action in the world. We are called to be ambassadors of forgiveness, seeking peace, justice, and reconciliation in our communities and beyond.

Practicing forgiveness has numerous benefits, not only for our emotional and spiritual well-being but also for our physical health. By letting go of anger, resentment, and the desire for revenge, we can experience greater empathy, compassion, and a willingness to seek reconciliation.

As we conclude this book, let us encourage one another to continue to practice forgiveness, knowing that it is a journey that requires patience, perseverance, and trust in the transformative power of God's grace. Let us be agents of healing and hope in a broken world, trusting that through our forgiveness, we can create a more peaceful and loving world, one relationship at a time.

Recap Of Key Points

In this book, we explored the topic of forgiveness from various angles, including its definition, benefits, challenges, and practical applications.

Here are some of the key points we covered:

- Forgiveness is the intentional decision to let go of anger, resentment, and the desire for revenge towards someone who has wronged us.
- Forgiveness is beneficial for both the forgiver and the forgiven, as it promotes emotional and physical health, improves relationships, and fosters inner peace.
- Forgiveness is not easy, as it requires vulnerability, courage, and a willingness to let go of control.
- Forgiveness does not mean excusing or forgetting the offense, nor does it always require reconciliation with the offender.
- Forgiveness can be practiced in various contexts, including personal relationships, community and social contexts, conflict resolution, and global conflicts.
- Forgiveness can be supported by various practices, such as acknowledging the hurt, choosing to forgive, letting go of anger and resentment, practicing empathy and compassion, seeking reconciliation (when possible), balancing forgiveness with healthy boundaries, and cultivating a forgiving spirit.
- Forgiveness is an important aspect of Christian faith, as it reflects the ultimate act of forgiveness by Jesus Christ on the cross.
- Forgiveness can contribute to healing emotional and physical wounds, as well as promoting spiritual growth.

Overall, forgiveness is a powerful and transformative

practice that can have significant positive impacts on individuals, relationships, communities, and even the world.

Final Thoughts on Forgiveness in the Christian Context.

Forgiveness is a central theme in the Christian faith, and it is rooted in the teachings of Jesus Christ. As Christians, we are called to forgive others as we have been forgiven by God. This is not always easy, but it is essential for our spiritual growth and our relationships with others.

Throughout this book, we have explored the many dimensions of forgiveness. We have looked at the importance of acknowledging hurt, choosing to forgive, letting go of anger and resentment, practicing empathy and compassion, seeking reconciliation, and balancing forgiveness with healthy boundaries. We have also considered the relationship between forgiveness and justice, the role of accountability, and the transformative power of forgiveness in personal, social, and global contexts.

As we conclude, I want to encourage you to practice forgiveness in your own life. Remember that forgiveness is a process that takes time and effort, but it is ultimately liberating and healing. Seek God's guidance and strength as you navigate the complexities of forgiveness, and know that you are not alone.

Finally, let us remember that forgiveness is not just a personal practice, but also a call to action in the world. As Christians, we are called to be ambassadors of forgiveness, seeking peace, justice, and reconciliation in our communities and beyond. Let us be agents of healing and hope in a broken world, trusting in the power of God's grace to transform lives and relationships.

ABOUT THE AUTHOR

Thelma Melissa Grey

Thelma is somewhere out there, living with her dog, contemplating about life.

BOOKS BY THIS AUTHOR

From Rage To Radiance: Mastering Anger Management For Women

From Rage to Radiance: Mastering Anger Management for Women

Do you ever feel like your anger gets in the way of your happiness and relationships? Are you tired of being told to just "calm down" or accused of being too emotional?

It's time to go from raging to radiant with this empowering guide for women. Discover how to identify your triggers, develop healthy coping mechanisms, and transform your anger into inner strength. With loads of techniques and practical advice, this book will help you reclaim your power and find inner peace. Say goodbye to the negative effects of anger and hello to a radiant, fulfilling life.

It's time to empower yourself and live your best life.